Dedication

To my beautiful Mother, Annette D. Walker.

The creator of this entrepreneurial spirit. Thank you for always uplifting and pushing me to become the original Purposeful Daughter. Thank you for instilling so many strong attributes into me from the time I was born, up until now. You're the reason I'm here to inspire others. I will live through you.

I Love You Mommy!

About the Author

Damica Deshay is a wife and a mother of two teenagers. She is a first-time self-published author from Las Vegas, NV. She's the Founder of her own non-profit organization known as the D.O.L.L.S. (Daughters Overcoming Life Lessons Successfully). She is a youth community advocate who's on a mission to change the narrative of young girls who feels lost with nowhere to turn.

Damica is a public speaker and mentor at multiple public schools throughout the city of Las Vegas and surrounding areas. She was appointed a Las Vegas Casa Advocate in February 2020 and is also now a Life Coach to many. Her journey is to continue to encourage the youth that their life is required, and that they need to live their life on purpose.

Table of Contents

Introduction	4
Who are you?	5
What is your purpose in life?	12
Who are you to others?	19
Parents	25
Love	33
Trust	40
Know Your Worth	47
Education	54
Social Media Etiquette	61
Bullying	68
Hygiene	75
Menstrual Cycle (Period)	83
Time Management	94
Credit/ Finances	100
Entrepreneurship	106
Being a Better You	112
Affirmations	136

Introduction

This book is for you! You have inspired me to remind you that you were never a mistake. You are meant to be here in this world on purpose. As you partake in this journey of life, you will push through every trial with a stride of confidence. You will realize that your imperfections are actually your perfections. You were created as a daughter on purpose.

You are a Purposeful Daughter.

Who are you?

Have you ever just looked in the mirror and asked yourself. "Who am I?" This is something you should do multiple times in your life because you will change as a person as the days go by. If you have never done this before, I urge you to stop what you are doing and go take a look in the mirror and ask yourself that same question. If you're not by a mirror, use your phone or use some form of a window that shows your reflection when you walk by. I do this often when I'm out walking around in a store, mall, and parking lot. Pretty much wherever I can see my reflection. Now when you are looking at yourself, I don't want you to look at just the exterior (outside), I want you to look at the interior (inside) as well. The most important thing is you are on the inside.

Now while looking at yourself, tell me 5 things you see or feel about yourself. I also want you to be honest because this is your journey. Ask yourself, how do you feel at this moment? Why do you feel this way? If you had a chance to change your feelings, what would you do? Did someone cause you to feel this way?

Try to change your feelings right now at this moment. Whether it's a good or bad feeling. Were you able to change it? Your answer should be yes. This means that you are in charge of your feelings.

However, I do want you to understand that other people can and will make you happy and unhappy. So, this is why I want you to practice becoming in control of your feelings.

There will be many days you will have to smile but deep down inside you want to cry. I want to let you know that it is ok to feel this way. And guess what? It's ok to cry. I myself have noticed that sometimes when you cry, you feel so much better inside. You are human and this too shall pass. There are always better days ahead. You just need to be a little patient. I promise.

Repeat after me:

I am a unique daughter of this world who is perfectly made.

I am happy to be here.

I have so much brightness inside me to light up the world at any given time.

I am living my life on purpose.

I am perfect just the way I am.

"My mission in life is not merely to survive, but to thrive; and to do so with some passion, some compassion, some humor, and some style."

– Maya Angelou

Let's Talk About It:

Tell me who you are right now in your life? Who do you want to be? Do you like the person you are right now? What steps are you going to take to be better? Do you promise to love you unconditionally?

_____
_____
_____
_____
_____
_____
_____
_____
_____
_____
_____
_____
_____
_____
_____
_____
_____
_____
_____
_____
_____
_____

Tape a Picture of You Here

Give yourself 3 compliments:

1.
2.
3.

What is Your Purpose in Life?

Your purpose in life is to do as much good as you can while you're here and live your life on purpose!

Have you ever wondered what you wanted to be when you grow up? As the years go by, you may change your mind and want to do something else. It is ok. Your heart and strength will determine your purpose. Remember that you have a reason to be here. The world needs you. Sometimes it may feel as if your whole world is coming down but that is just a temporary feeling. You will need to learn how to channel the negative energy into positive energy. When you're going through a hard time, take a breath and think about the things that make you happy and try to remember things that have happened in the past and made you happy. It won't fix what you're going through, but it will distract you temporarily and help you to calm down.

You were born as someone's Princess and your purpose is to walk through life willing to listen, learn and participate in making you a Queen. You have to be eager and willing to learn from others. You want to observe the good and the bad types of people that you want and don't want to be compared to.

You must be open to listening to others and their stories. You'll be surprised how much you can learn from a person or about a person just by learning to listen well. I remember I heard a saying that said, "Are you listening to reply or are you listening to understand." When you are listening to reply, you don't really hear what the other person is saying because you are thinking of how to reply. Now, when you're listening to understand, it is just that. You're trying to understand the speaker.

From this day forward, I want you to trust the process in your life. Believe that dreams do come true. I never would have thought people would be reading my thoughts and prayers. Now look, you don't know me, and I don't know you but you're reading my words. I hope that they are encouraging to you and assist you through finding your purpose. Having a purpose in your life is the key to your happiness.

Repeat after me:

My life is meaningful.

My dreams are achievable.

I am a gigantic gift to this world.

I will live my life on purpose.

I am somebody.

I love me so much that I will never give up on myself.

"No one is you, and that is your superpower!"

– Elyse Santilli

Let's Talk About It:

Tell me what you believe your purpose in life is? How will you start achieving this goal? Who else can help you start moving forward with this purpose?

_____
_____
_____
_____
_____
_____
_____
_____
_____
_____
_____
_____
_____
_____
_____
_____
_____
_____
_____
_____
_____
_____
_____
_____
_____
_____

Tape a Picture of You Here

Give yourself 3 compliments:

1.
2.
3.

Who Are You to Others?

Have you ever wondered how other people perceive you? Often, we say that we don't care what others may think of us. But in reality, is this true? We do care what others think. It may not truly change your life in most cases, but it can build character within you.

You have to understand that everyone won't like you and you won't like everyone you encounter. I'm not saying that you will hate them, but this is just life. There will be many people that will judge you from your past. Please keep in mind that there will always be someone who doesn't want you to grow as a person. Therefore, they will bring up your past faults. But guess what, who cares! You are living your life for YOU, not them.

What you want to focus on, is leaving a positive impression on the people you encounter throughout your beautiful life. Whether it be old or new friends, family or strangers. Always do your best to be kind to others because you never know when you may cross paths with them again. Like they can end up being your boss, your professor, your teammate, your doctor or coworker.

So always make sure when leaving someone's presence, you leave them feeling good about you and themselves.

Repeat after me:

I am beautiful, smart and kind.

I am a good listener.

I show compassion in helping others when needed.

I am a friend.

I am here to stay; the world needs me.

"I've learned that people will forget what you said, people will forget what you did, but people will never forget how you made them feel."

– Maya Angelou

Let's Talk About It:

Tell me what do you think others think of you? Is there someone in particular that you want them to think differently of you? Why? What will you do to change their mind?

Tape a Picture of You Here

Give yourself 3 compliments:

1.
2.
3.

Parents

When speaking on parents it could be your actual parents, foster parents or adoptive parents. It means the adult figure who is currently taking care of you to the best of their ability. I want you to understand that these are the people that you want to put all your trust in. You should build a relationship with your parents so that you can talk about almost anything. This will be one of the most important relationships you will have. It is with your parents.

I know that there are some situations when you can't tell them certain things, but I do want you to at least try. Your parents are here on this earth to protect you at any cost. Yes, they do understand that mistakes will be made by you and them, but you all must be open to correct them and move on.

At times, I know it may be hard to talk to your parents or tell them some things, but what I want you to remember is that they were kids too! I'm sure that they have made mistakes like you. Some may have even been worse than you think. Parents are the ones who are going to give you that tough love and try to save you from the outside world. You have to be careful because people will try and manipulate you to get what they want. It may sound good at the time, but it can turn out bad.

Sometimes parents can seem like they are being very strict about your friends and your life. Have you ever heard of something called an intuition? It's a feeling you get inside without using reasoning or perception. It's like a snap judgment feeling. It's something that we all have. But for parents a radar when you bring certain friends around and they instantly know that they aren't a good fit for you. I want you to please trust your parents when this happens. I'm not saying just cut the friend off. I'm saying be very cautious when interacting with them. If you have to question yourself every time you all hang out, then yes, that is not the friend for you.

In some cases, I know that it can be difficult to communicate with a parent. Maybe they aren't home, don't like to talk, are always busy or just flat out mean. This doesn't mean you still can't talk or communicate with them. You can always write them a letter or a sticky note and leave it where they can find it. They might just write on the back or come and talk to you.

It's now time that you get comfortable with communication and speaking up for yourself. These types of values will get you through a lot of things in the future. You always want to communicate verbally instead of physically. It will be frustrating sometimes because nobody understands but don't give up. Speak up. Your family will be your support system. They will be there forever.

Occasionally, your parents may not be your "real" parents, but they love you just like your biological parents should. Just remember you are not responsible for adults making bad choices. These are the times when foster or adoptive parents step in to help take care of you. Make sure you treat them with respect and love as well. Again, you must communicate when things are bothering you. Nobody will understand what you are going through unless you tell them. Even if you are in a foster home and things aren't going as expected. Guess who needs to speak up? YOU! This is your life. You are in charge of your destiny. You have to remember to always be respectful when you are expressing yourself. Even if you're angry. I know that when you are in foster care or going through the adoption process there are always caseworkers assigned to your case. If you can't talk to your foster or adoptive parents, talk to your caseworker. Verbally express the situations that aren't going right in your life. It will only make your life easier.

What are some things parents don't understand? Can you talk to them to help them understand? Yes, you can. So, at the end of this chapter, write down some things you want to talk to your parents about, but you are afraid. Then write down a date and time you want to tell them. Now make sure you keep that meeting to talk to them. Ok?

Repeat after me:

I will trust my parents with my secrets.

I will speak up for myself in the most respected way.

My parents are my protectors.

I will communicate with my parents with all the things I go through.

I am here to stay; the world needs me.

My parents love me.

I can talk to my parents about anything.

I will make myself and my parents proud.

"If you're not going to speak up, how is the world supposed to know you exist?"

- Unknown

Let's Talk About It:

What are some of the things you would like to talk to your parents about? Are your parents easy to talk to? What are some ways you can communicate with your parents to make things easier?

_____
_____
_____
_____
_____
_____
_____
_____
_____
_____
_____
_____
_____
_____
_____
_____
_____
_____
_____
_____
_____
_____
_____
_____

Tape a Picture of You Here

Give yourself 3 compliments:

1.
2.
3.

Love

Love can mean so many different things. You can have a love for people, animals, clothes, shoes, and places. However, love and infatuation are two different things. You can be romantically in love which means you combined attraction and closeness with someone. Attraction without being close to someone is more like infatuation or just simply a crush.

You want to be careful when using the word love towards a person. Some things I want you to understand about love is that you don't want to justify that you love someone just by their charming looks, money, attitude and because they are popular. You want to get to know a person well before you try to have feelings for them. You will never know who or when you'll fall in love but just be cautious of people and them trying to manipulate you.

There will be times when you may think that you may have fallen in love and this may be true, but just be cautious of moving so fast. You don't ever want to rush love. You have to make sure that the person you're falling in love with respects you, your parents and your decisions. A person who loves you wants the best for you. A person who loves you won't lie to you. A person who loves you will keep you safe and out of trouble. A person who loves you will respect your parents. A person who loves you will never ever hit you! A person who loves you will never talk bad to you and make you feel small. You will never have to question yourself or that person if you're sure that you both love each other. Their actions will prove their love, not only their words. To give love, you have to love yourself first.

Repeat after me:

I approve of myself.

I deserve to be treated with love and respect.

Love is not one-sided.

Love isn't supposed to hurt.

I am here to stay; the world needs me.

I love me. I am awesome!

Love is kind.

Love is deserving.

"Waiting is a sign of true love and patience. Anyone can say I love you, but not everyone can wait and prove it's true."

-Unknown

Let's Talk About It:

What is love to you? Do you think love hurts? If so, how? Have you ever been in love? Do you love yourself? Why or why not?

**Tape a Picture of You
or Someone You Love Here**

Give yourself 3 compliments:

1.
2.
3.

Trust

What is trust? The dictionary version of trust is a firm belief in the reliability, truth, ability, or strength of someone or something. Now let's break it down so you can understand. When you think of trust do you think of secrets?
Your inner thoughts? Parents? Family and friends?

You always want to be a trusted friend. You want to build your character as a person where others will confide in you and trust you with their secrets. You always want to be the person who has strong confidence in being trustworthy.

I know sometimes it can be hard to trust people when they have told your secrets or maybe even lied about you. But don't give up on people. Everyone is not the same and we all make mistakes. You just want to be mindful of trusting the same person over and over again.

Some people that should be on your top trust list are your parents! You should be able to trust them with all of your secrets. Even the ones that you think you may get in trouble for. Your parents should be the first to know especially if it's something bad. When you think that there is nothing nobody can do for you, I can almost promise you they will have a way to make things right all over again.

Let me say this, strangers could be very dangerous. With all the things that are happening in the world today, I would say hold off on trusting strangers. You don't know them. Never go anywhere alone with strangers. Don't ever go meet strangers you've met online because most of the time they are not who they say they are. Always be careful who you give your information to like where you live or your name because people may try to follow you.

I am not trying to scare you; I just want you to know that trusting people can cost you your life. So always tell someone where you are going and who you are with. Just for extra safety.

Repeat after me:

I trust myself.

I can trust my parents.

I honor and trust myself with every decision I make.

I am an inspiration to my friends and family

I am here to stay the world needs me.

I will trust my intuition thoughts.

I am trustworthy.

I trust myself to make the right decisions to be happy.

"The future belongs to those who believe in the beauty of their dreams."

– Eleanor Roosevelt

Let's Talk About It:

Who do you trust? Why do you trust them? Do you have a secret that you're afraid to tell? What is it? Who do you think you can trust with that secret? When are you going to tell them about it?

**Tape a Picture of You
or Someone You Love Here**

Give yourself 3 compliments:

1.
2.
3.

Know Your Worth

Have you ever heard the saying know your worth? It doesn't have a monetary value, but it does have a great amount of self-value. To understand your worth, you have to know your strengths and weaknesses. Ask yourself some personal questions that only you can answer. You have to learn from your mistakes. Reflect on what happened, how it worked out and the outcome of it. Was it worth it? What did you learn?

Knowing your worth is an amazing feeling. When you are put into a situation you have to know that you are equal to anyone you interact with. Whether it's your friends, family, clients, and classmates. Meaning your life is just as valuable as theirs.

Understanding your worth and value is essential if you want to have success and happiness in your life. For you to feel completely alive, you must have a strong sense of self-worth and acquire confidence. The more you believe in yourself, the well-organized and successful you'll be in all aspects of your life.

Many people will tell you to "forget it, it's in the past." I say, learn from the things that happened in your past. The things you overcome from your past just make your future look brighter and more fulfilling. This is why you want to be careful as well as what others think about you. Life is too short to dwell on what other people think of you. Sometimes you want to understand why people don't like you or think so negatively of you, but that just drains you. Just think if they focused on themselves more than they focused on you, then maybe they wouldn't have the time to talk about you. The most important thing is your opinion of yourself! Think of things you can do for yourself to grow and do better in life.

You have to approve of yourself before you can expect others too. Take a look in the mirror every chance you get to see your reflection. Not just of your looks but also what's inside of you. Believe in yourself above all else. You are what's important to you. Remember that anything that awakens your passion fuels your value. We are who we believe we are. So that just means we need to give ourselves a pep talk when we're feeling down or weak. Now, you can always ask those you've worked with or friends what value do they see in you. Never be afraid to take constructive criticism. This will allow you to work on the things you need to look inside yourself to fix.

All these will assist you in becoming a better you and finding your worth. You may not find it right away but just pay attention to your surroundings and the things you take personally. Everything isn't meant for you to hold on too. Take the lesson out of it and move on. Remember, you are the most important in your life. People need YOU!

Repeat after me:

I am unique in my talents and abilities and I do not need validation from others.

I love and accept myself for who I am.

I am a unique and a very special person.

I am worthy of all the good things that happen in my life.

I acknowledge my self-worth and know that my self-confidence is rising.

I am living my life on purpose.

"Know your worth, hold your own power, be you."

– Morgan Harper Nichols

Let's Talk About It:

What makes you feel good about yourself? What are some things you will and will not tolerate in your life? What are you worth? What are the things you value about yourself?

_____
_____
_____
_____
_____
_____
_____
_____
_____
_____
_____
_____
_____
_____
_____
_____
_____
_____
_____
_____
_____
_____
_____
_____
_____

**Tape a Picture of You
or Someone You Love Here**

Give yourself 3 compliments:

1.
2.
3.

Education

As you know education is a vital aspect of your life. It is required because you need to gain skills, knowledge, and values to help you throughout life. You can't get through life if you can't read, write or count. That just means that you will have to depend on and trust people with your entire life. This is why you need to learn these things on your own so you can be independent and live on your own. Education can and will improve your personal life and even those around you.

Sometimes it may seem like school is the hardest thing ever. And it could be, but what I want you to remember is that the teachers are paid to help you through the hard times. You can raise your hand and ask as many questions as you like if you don't understand the lesson being taught. If you are shy and afraid to ask your question in front of others, you can always write a note to the teacher and place it on their desk. You also can request to stay after school to get some extra help. I know sometimes it can be hard to get the attention you need from a teacher, so just make sure you know that you can always talk to your parents or a school counselor as well for additional help.

While you are getting an education in school, there are also other valuable lessons to be learned at home and outside of your home. Your parents will teach you great things like how to express yourself with respect, keeping yourself clean and fresh, maintaining a clean house, how to cook, how to love and many other things. So, don't just think that you can only learn at school. There are so many other places and people you can learn from. You can also learn from other people's mistakes. When you see that someone has gotten in trouble for something they did, you will make a mental note of it and tell yourself you won't make that same mistake. That's a part of education as well. Just remember, the more education you receive the more you will increase your opportunities in life. So, learn something every chance you get. Nothing is too small.

Repeat after me:

If I can conceive it and believe it, I can achieve it.

Mistakes won't stop me; they will help me grow.

I will complete my education to fulfill my dreams.

I realize that this is the age to study and prepare for the future and I am doing so sincerely.

I am living my life on purpose.

I am smart.

I will ask questions when I don't understand.

I won't give up on me.

Listening to others can teach me from making the same mistakes.

"I was surrounded by extraordinary women in my life who taught me about quiet strength and dignity."

– Michelle Obama

Let's Talk About It:

Is education important to you? Do you want to go to college? Do you like school? Are you afraid to ask questions? If so, why?

_____
_____
_____
_____
_____
_____
_____
_____
_____
_____
_____
_____
_____
_____
_____
_____
_____
_____
_____
_____
_____
_____
_____
_____
_____

**Tape a Picture of You
or Someone You Love Here**

Give yourself 3 compliments:

1.
2.
3.

Social Media Etiquette

Let's be real, social media is a big thing these days. Almost everyone has one. Now let's talk about the things that we shouldn't put on social media. I'm sure you already have an idea of the things that should not be posted, but we're going to discuss them anyway.

Nude or partially nude photos and videos of you or anyone else.

Fights of you or anyone else.

Please don't ever bully anyone via social media. (Would you want to be bullied?) Don't post anything you wouldn't want your parents, teachers, judges or anyone you admire, or respect see. Just think, you may be embarrassed some years from now.

Being disrespectful verbally or physically to anyone. Now, there may be many other topics and things you shouldn't post or share but these are the ones that are the most important to me at this time. Social media is everywhere. So, one thing you have to remember about the internet is that when you put it out there, you can't erase it.

Imagine you post a nude or partially nude photo of yourself. Then you decide you changed your mind and delete it. Guess what, somebody already took a screenshot of it and reposted it. Now, what do you do? You can ask them to take it down but imagine how many other people already saw it and took a screenshot. Now you don't know who may have it on their phone or computer. Now let's say you posted or shared a nude or partially nude picture of someone else. Now let's think about this, if they're under the age of 18, you are now sharing and posting child pornography. You can be prosecuted and in really big trouble for doing that. The fight you posted is your new teacher or boss's daughter. How would you feel? How would you explain your actions if asked? The person you were bullying decided to commit suicide. Can you live with that?

These are the truths and facts that can simply happen from putting things on social media. So please, if you do have a social media account, think before you post. Will this harm my future?

Repeat after me:

I am a leader and not a follower.

I understand that my actions become habits, so I will try to do the right thing.

I will be respectful to myself and others.

I am here to stay; the world needs me.

My body is a masterpiece. I will respect it at all times.

"I am no longer accepting the things I cannot change. I am changing the things I cannot accept."

- Angela Davis

Let's Talk About It:

Can you recall a time when you or a friend posted something on social media and after it posted it you all wanted to change your mind? Did anyone see it and you didn't want them too? Have you ever got in trouble about something on social media? Do you regret it? If you don't have a social media account, what are some things you will never post? Do you think you can encourage a friend not to post certain things on social media? Do your part and be a leader!

_____
_____
_____
_____
_____
_____
_____
_____
_____
_____
_____
_____
_____
_____
_____
_____
_____
_____
_____
_____

**Tape a Picture of You
or Someone You Love Here**

Give yourself 3 compliments:

1.
2.
3.

Bullying

What is bullying? Bullying is unwanted and aggressive behavior towards someone. Bullies seek to harm, intimidate and sometimes even coerce others to do things that they are not comfortable doing. This can be a very touchy subject. I know that we have all seen, heard or watched someone get bullied. Whether it was in person or online. When you see it, you get a gut feeling inside your body knowing it's not right. When you get that feeling, it just means that you know it's wrong. A bully is something I NEVER want you to be!

I want you to be mindful of bullies. Honestly, they are not all bad people. Sometimes people go through a lot of things at home or within themselves and they don't know how to deal with it. So, therefore, they will take it out on someone else. Which isn't the right thing to do, but they don't know how else to handle it. If you ever see anyone getting bullied. Please get an adult immediately. You don't want to jump in the middle of it because then the bully might try to attack you. So, you want to be careful and get help. It may be times when you don't see it but you can hear it or you have seen a video. I still want you to report it. If it were you, wouldn't you want someone to help you?

Always report any physical abuse whether it's a child, friend, parent or stranger. If you ever see someone getting abused, don't be afraid to call for help. Being bullied is not a great feeling. Some people can't handle it and they will take their own life. This is something you don't want to be responsible for.

So, this means you will always be kind and look out for others.

Repeat after me:

I will not be a bully.

I will not get bullied.

I will not allow others to get bullied around me.

I will inform a respected adult if I witness or hear anyone getting bullied.

I am perfectly made, and nobody can change my mind.

"If you turn and face the other way when someone is being bullied, you might as well be the bully too."

- Unknown

Let's Talk About It:

Are you a bully? Do you know someone who is being bullied? Are you being bullied? If so, by whom? Who do you think you can tell if you're getting bullied? Think of an adult that will help you out if you need to report bullying.

Who is it?

_____
_____
_____
_____
_____
_____
_____
_____
_____
_____
_____
_____
_____
_____
_____
_____
_____
_____
_____
_____

**Tape a Picture of You
or Someone You Love Here**

Give yourself 3 compliments:

1.
2.
3.

Hygiene

What is hygiene? Hygiene are conditions or practices conducive to maintaining health and preventing disease, especially through cleanliness.

Now that's the dictionary version of what hygiene is. Let's break it down. Hygiene is saying we need to do our best at keeping our bodies clean. We have to try and make sure we shower or wash up at least once a day if you can. Let's be honest, everyone may not have their own personal shower or bathtub to take a full shower or bath. If you find yourself in a situation where you don't have a shower or bathtub, try to get you a towel or cloth to wash up with.

When you are cleaning your body, you want to make sure you clean your entire body. However, again there may be times when you just have to wash the "important parts." So, what will be the important parts?

Face- Your face is important because dirt, germs, and sweat are easily accumulated to the skin on your face. After all, it is the most exposed throughout the day. Be cautious when you're trying to pick or touch your zits because it will leave a scar. It may even possibly spread more bacteria across the face. So, try to not aggravate them as much.

Teeth- You want to brush and floss your teeth at least twice a day to keep away germs, cavities and to keep a fresh breath.

Armpits- Gently wash your underarms daily with a mild soap to reduce the growth of smelly bacteria. When you reach your teen years or puberty, it becomes necessary to wear deodorant or antiperspirant so that you can keep smelling fresh all day long. Choose a deodorant or antiperspirant that you like. Make sure to read the label to make sure it's the right one for you. Apply a couple swipes to each underarm unless the label says otherwise. Deodorant is used to control the smell of body odor while antiperspirants help you to not sweat as much. If you sweat a lot, look for a deodorant that contains an antiperspirant. There are two types of deodorants: the stick type or you can get the spray-on deodorant.

Buttocks- It is very important to clean your behind because we all know what comes out of there. While in the shower you simply turn your back to the water and allow the water to rinse it first. You can spread your cheeks gently to allow a full complete rinse. Once you've rinsed it you can use your cloth with soap and water to give it a real great cleanse. Once it's cleaned with soap make sure to repeat the rinse process.

Private Area- Now when cleaning your girly private area always make sure to be gentle. You do not want to put soap inside of that area. Make sure to clean the lips and around the area with a mild unscented soap. Rinse well and pat dry. There is something called a pH Balance inside of our bodies. It is pretty much the level of acids and bases in your blood at which your body functions best. The human body is built to naturally maintain a healthy balance of acidity and alkalinity. So as a young lady, you don't want to put things inside that will mess up the pH balance inside of your body.

Feet- You may not think that your feet are not a big deal but guess what, they do smell. You should always wash your feet. Regularly washing the skin on your feet, the top, sides, and bottom should be washed with soap and water.

This is an easy way to stop them from smelling.

These are the main things that should be an everyday regimen to stay clean and fresh. Some other things you may want to consider are to wash all of your clothes before wearing them again.

If you are unable to use a washer and dryer you can wash them in a sink by hand and hang them up to dry. Remember to never share hairbrushes, combs, makeup, and drinks. These items can also spread plenty of germs. Everything isn't meant to be shared.

Repeat after me:

I am developing the mindset of someone who is effortlessly clean and hygienic.

I love to smell fresh and clean.

Keeping everything clean is an important part of my life.

It is important to me that my house and room be clean and healthy.

By staying clean, it can also clear my mind.

I will live a happy and clean life.

I will maintain a clean body and heart.

"Good hygiene enhanced sound well-being."

- Lailah Gifty Akita

Let's Talk About It:

Do you try to keep good hygiene? What are some things you will be working on for good hygiene? Do you keep hygiene products in your backpack or purse for emergencies?

**Tape a Picture of You
or Someone You Love Here**

Give yourself 3 compliments:

1.
2.
3.

Menstrual Cycle (Period)

As a young lady, we have been given the luxury of having something called a menstruation period. What is Menstruation? Per the dictionary: it is also known as a period or monthly. It is a regular discharge of blood and mucosal tissue (known as menses) from the inner lining of the uterus through the vagina. The monthly cycle of changes in the ovaries and the lining of the uterus (endometrium), starting with the preparation of an egg for fertilization.

Each month, one of the ovaries releases an egg. This is called ovulation. When ovulation takes place and the egg is not fertilized, the lining of the uterus sheds and drains through the vagina. This is called a menstruation cycle or a period.

Try not to feel embarrassed talking about your period. This is a natural thing that every girl goes through, and it's normal to have questions about how to deal with it. I know when you first start your cycle, you feel as if everyone who walks by you just knows. Lol. Nope, they honestly won't have a clue if you just take the precautions to keep yourself clean and prepared. Most of us can get emotional around this time of the month, so try to remember that. There are times when you just want to cry. Lol. Go ahead. It's ok. You might even want to yell. Go ahead, it's ok. Just as long as you're not yelling at someone. At this time of the month, you have to be careful about how you react to others as well.

Now we'll never know the exact age when we will start our period, but we want to be ready when it's our turn. When you first start your period, you may see a small amount of brown drainage in your underwear or on the toilet paper. Don't be alarmed, this is normal.

A lot of young ladies want to know will it hurt when you get your period. All of our bodies are different. Some of you may experience some cramps at the bottom of your stomach. Some physicians will say exercise is recommended to increase the blood flow to the uterus. You can ask your parents to get you some over-the-counter medicine for cramps and menstrual cycle symptoms or get a heating pad to help with the discomfort with the help of a parent.

If you are new to a period or just recently started, you can also track your cycle. I know if you have a cell phone several apps can help you keep track. Some are free as well, so be sure to check with a parent to make sure you're not being charged. Just know that it is normal for your period to be irregular for the first year or two. Everyone's body is different, so you will have your own personal cycle monthly. Therefore, it's a good idea to keep track of a calendar.

Feminine Hygiene Product

Now let's talk about sanitary pads and tampons. Decide which products you like best and choose the ones that you're most comfortable using. I will suggest you speak with a parent or health professional before using tampons. If you've gotten your period recently, you may want to use pads, which just stick right in your underwear as a liner. Tampons are a good choice if you'll be swimming or have to wear tight clothes for sports, as they're inserted inside the vagina. I would consider using a pad while you sleep. It may be more comfortable. When choosing your pad or tampon, pay close attention to the different labels on pads and tampons. Some are for regular flow, while others are intended for heavier flows, so choose the one that most describes your period. It may vary for some months. It's up to you to keep track and pay attention to your flow. To understand more about using pads and tampons, you can always read the instructions that come with your package or ask a trusted adult or friend for help.

You should change your pad or tampon approximately every 3-4 hours to keep yourself fresh and healthy. This is especially important if you're using a tampon. However, I do understand that things happen, and you may not be able to change that often, so the maximum amount of time is about

8 hours some sources say. Now keep in mind that when wearing tampons, you don't want to keep them in longer than 8 hours because you can cause toxic shock syndrome and make yourself sick. Just try to be cautious and clean.

How to Change Your Feminine Hygiene Product

To change your pad, simply remove the pad from your underwear. If it has wings, remove the wings from the bottom of your underwear and then remove the pad. Roll up your pad to dispose of it. Now replace it with a new one. You can also take the wrapper from the new one and place the old pad inside the wrapper.

To remove your tampon, there is a string that should be hanging down. Simply use two fingers (index & thumb) to gently pull it out. You can wrap it in some tissue or wrap it in the new wrapper that you just got from the new tampon.

Now it's time to dispose of the products safely and hygienically. There are some places at schools and public restrooms that have bathrooms with feminine hygiene disposal containers inside of the stall. Once you wrap it up, you can place it inside that box. If there aren't any, just dispose of it in the trash. Make sure you wash your hands before and after changes.

Be sure to keep an emergency kit in your locker, purse or backpack at that time of the month or if you know the time is near. In your emergency kit, you should have an extra pair of clean underwear, extra pads or tampons, and wipes. Always try to wear dark-colored bottoms or you can tie a sweatshirt around your waist to cover that area if you are not feeling too comfortable. If you have a locker at school, it's always a good idea to keep an extra pair of jeans, a dress or skirt in there as well just in case. If you have any additional questions, you can always talk to a trusted adult about your period, like which products are best to use, how you use them, or what to do if you run out while you're at school.

Repeat after me:

I accept my full power as a woman and accept all my bodily processes as natural and normal.

I love and approve of myself.

I trust the process of life.

Menstruation does not affect my well-being.

I was created to endure this journey as a young woman.

I am normal.

I was created with a purpose.

"Every time my period comes, I rejoice in the fact that my body is functioning correctly."

- Unknown

Let's Talk About It:

Have you started your period yet? Did this chapter teach you anything? Do you have additional questions you want to ask? What are they? Do you feel better about having your period? Did you know that you are Awesome!

_____
_____
_____
_____
_____
_____
_____
_____
_____
_____
_____
_____
_____
_____
_____
_____
_____
_____
_____
_____
_____
_____
_____

**Tape a Picture of You
or Someone You Love Here**

Give yourself 3 compliments:

1.
2.
3.

Time Management

While going through life, we have to make sure that our time is utilized wisely. We have to make sure we respect other people's time as they should ours. When you have an appointment, make it your duty to leave early to make sure you make it on time.

You will be respected more when you respect people's time. Always do your best to get to school on time. This will allow you to be prepared before class begins. Be on time to work. This will allow you to get mentally prepared before your shift begins. Be on time for your appointments. This will give you additional time just in case you need to fill out paperwork, get through traffic or pass any other issue that may occur that will make you late.

I want you to realize that you also need some time to yourself. Sometimes we need to sit and have alone time to regroup mentally. Your mental health is just as important as your actual health. You want to give yourself some time to think about how things are going in your life and what you need to change. Always remember self-care.

Repeat after me:

Every day I make more time for the things and people I love.

Every minute of my day is dynamic and productive.

I am excellent at time management.

I am motivated to stick to my plans.

I am living my life on purpose.

I will be on time to all of my appointments.

I will respect other people's time.

"Yesterday is gone. Tomorrow has not yet come. We have only today. Let us begin."

- Mother Teresa

Let's Talk About It:

Do you value your time? Do you use your time wisely? Do you waste other people's time? Are you always late for something?

_____
_____
_____
_____
_____
_____
_____
_____
_____
_____
_____
_____
_____
_____
_____
_____
_____
_____
_____
_____
_____
_____
_____
_____

**Tape a Picture of You
or Someone You Love Here**

Give yourself 3 compliments:

1.
2.
3.

Credit/ Finances

I know you're thinking that you're too young to think about credit and finances but you're not. I won't get too complex about it. I just want you to know that these things will be very important in your adulthood. So, if you learn bits and pieces and ask questions now, it will make sense in your future.

Also, if you're over the age of 15, ask your parents if they can add you to their credit cards if they have good credit. This way, when you reach the age of 18, which you are now considered an adult, you would be able to start your adulthood with a good credit score. The standard credit range is 300-850. With 850 being the highest score. Keep an eye on your credit as you get older. You got this!

Repeat after me:

I am financially free.

I have a positive relationship with money and know-how to spend it wisely.

I choose to live rich with my heart and money and have a full life.

I have the power to create success and build the wealth I desire.

I am wealthy in more ways than one.

I am responsible.

I will create great spending habits.

I will learn to invest.

"Friends and good manners will carry you where money won't go."

– Margaret Walker

Let's Talk About It:

What do you already know about credit? Do your parents have good or bad credit? Do you know how to save? What credit score do you need to buy a house? Do you need credit cards? Why or why not? Are you saving money right now?

_____
_____
_____
_____
_____
_____
_____
_____
_____
_____
_____
_____
_____
_____
_____
_____
_____
_____
_____
_____
_____
_____
_____
_____

**Tape a Picture of You
or Someone You Love Here**

Give yourself 3 compliments:

1.
2.
3.

Entrepreneurship

What is entrepreneurship? The dictionary version says: it's the activity of setting up a business or businesses, taking on financial risks in the hope of profit. I do understand that not everyone wants to own a business which is ok. Just make sure you follow the dreams of your heart.

I want you to know that the option is there for us women and young ladies. If you have the opportunity to google it, look and see how many women have their own business. That can be you as well. Just think, you don't have to be an adult to become an entrepreneur. Many kids have started their own businesses as well. Think about lemonade stands and yard sales. Kids create these all the time to make some extra money. So, you know what that means? It means that they have already started their own businesses. You can too! You can get with your parents, family, and friends for help and make it happen.

Write down any ideas you may have or something you want to do. A product you want to sell. Think of something others need and then you can figure out how to sell it. Technology is really big these days and you can think of different things you can do as well. You can create apps, websites, and flyers for businesses. That can make you some extra cash and help you become your own boss. The possibilities are endless. Go for it! #GirlPower

Repeat after me:

I have the potential and capabilities to run my own business.

I am a magnet for success.

I let myself move with confidence in the direction of my goals.

I feel confident that I can achieve anything I set my mind to.

I am an entrepreneur!

I will create careers for the future.

I am a leader.

I am able.

"You've just got to follow your own path. You have to trust your heart and you have to listen to the warnings."

– Chaka Khan

Let's Talk About It:

Do you have a business idea? What is it? What can you do to start the business? Who do you think can help you start the business? Why is your business required in the world? Start writing down the items you will need to get going.

_____
_____
_____
_____
_____
_____
_____
_____
_____
_____
_____
_____
_____
_____
_____
_____
_____
_____
_____
_____
_____
_____
_____

**Tape a Picture of You
or Someone You Love Here**

Give yourself 3 compliments:

1.
2.
3.

Being a Better You

Remember there is always room for self-improvement. We all make mistakes. Some can change our lives forever and some can be a temporary change. What we want to gain from it is the lesson we learned from it. Sometimes you won't be able to foresee the mistakes or try to put them in perspective beforehand. But what I want you to always do is remember how you felt at the time of the mistake, just so you don't want to feel that same way in the future.

In life, you won't be able to make everyone happy or make everyone like you. The most important thing is that you need to love yourself. Keep yourself happy. Focus on the people and things that make you happy. Treating others with respect and being kind does make you feel good inside. You don't have to always display your good deeds. You show good character about yourself when you do a good deed from the heart and don't have to brag about it. Sometimes, if you want to share certain things you can and should. Just make sure you always get others permission before you put them on any social media site.

After you finish this book/ journal, I want you to use it as a reference to come back to. See how you have grown, look at the changes in your life, help others through life the best you can and never give up on you. You were chosen to be the divine daughter you are. You don't have to change because others want you too, change because you want to be a better you. Every day I want you to compliment yourself. If you're having a hard day, go to the affirmations page in this book and just start residing affirmations. Repeat them over and over and throughout the day to keep yourself motivated. You'll find that this will make you feel like the better part of you.

Never forget, YOU are meant to be here in this world. We need you.
You are required to live your life on purpose!
I Love You!

Repeat after me:

I am love. I am purposeful. I was made with divine intention.

I can. I will. End of story.

I am in charge of how I feel and today I am choosing happiness.

I am choosing and not waiting to be chosen.

I belong here, the world needs me.

I will help those who need me the best way I can.

I am meant to be me.

I can always change to become a better me.

"Nothing makes a woman more beautiful than the belief that she is beautiful."

- Sophia Loren

Let's Talk About It:

What are some things you think you need to change about yourself? How do you think you could become a better daughter? How do you think you could be a better friend? Tell me your best affirmation you would like to tell yourself every day.

**Tape a Picture of You
or Someone You Love Here**

Give yourself 3 compliments:

1.
2.
3.

GOALS

What are your short-term goals?

What are your long-term goals?

What are your lifetime goals?

What would you like to be when you are older? Why?

What don't you want to be when you are older?

Affirmations

What are affirmations?

Everything that we repeatedly say to ourselves out loud or in our thoughts is an affirmation. When you do this consistently, eventually the negative self-talk will become a thing of the past. And you will feel good about yourself and your life.

Remember, the subconscious mind benefits from positive affirmations.
You must meditate on your affirmations. Close your eyes and think of your confirmation and the positive feeling you're trying to change

When you want to give up:

I press on because I believe in my path.

The world needs me. I belong here.

I'm strong enough to ask someone for help or support.

Someone admires you.

I see beauty in everything.

I easily accomplish all of my goals.

Everyone sees how much joy and love I have for life.

I crave new, healthy experiences.

Life wants the best for me. I am OK with where I am right now.

Your path is more difficult because your calling is higher.

Add your own affirmations for when you want to give up:

When you feel lonely:

I love and approve of myself.

I feel the love of those who are not physically around me.

I am grateful for what I have even if it's not perfect.

I attract positive people into my life.

I am surrounded by peaceful people.

My life is full of magic and serendipity.

I am present at every moment.

I am enthusiastic about every second of my life.

You inspire people who pretend to not even see you.

Trust yourself.

Add affirmations for when you feel lonely:

When you are losing confidence:

I listen to my heart.

I am confident.

I am allowed to feel proud of myself.

I am brave.

I am important.

I am strong.

I believe in myself.

I am awesome.

I trust myself.

Add affirmations for when you lose confidence:

When you lack self-love:

I accept myself.

I deserve to be happy.

I speak to myself with kindness.

I don't need to be perfect.

I forgive myself for all of my mistakes.

I accept my flaws.

I love myself.

I am worthy.

I love and accept all parts of myself.

Add affirmations for when you lack self-love:

When you are feeling scared:

Following my intuition and my heart keeps me safe and sound.

I focus on breathing and grounding myself.

All is well in my world and I am safe.

I overcome my fear of anything and everything and live life courageously.

I can accomplish anything I put my mind to because I know I'm never alone.

I am always joyful. For me, life is beautiful, wonderful and peaceful.

Every cell in my body is relaxed and oozes confidence.
The future is good. I look towards it with hope and happiness.

Life is wonderful. I trust in God/Universe to live a well fulfilled life.

I am strong.

Add affirmations for when you are scared:

For compassion:

I am generous.

I help others every chance I get.

I include others to make them feel accepted.

I am grateful for what I have.

I do my best to consider others feelings.

I won't judge others for their flaws.

I am compassionate.

I am kind.

Add more affirmations for compassion:

When you are angry:

BREATHE.

I am in charge of my happiness. I will not let anything outside of myself control me.

Don't live your life with anger and hate in your heart.

As long as I keep my cool, I'm in control of myself.

Each time I choose peace of mind over anger, my life gets better.

I transcend stress of any kind. I live in peace.

With every breath, I release the anxiety within me, and I become more and more calm.

My challenges bring me better opportunities.

My mood creates a physiological response in my body. I am peaceful and positive!

BREATHE.

Add affirmations for when you are feeling angry:

Love the skin you're in:

I love my body.

My body is strong and healthy.

I am beautiful.

My body is perfect the way it is.

I will respect my body at all times.

I will not compare my body to others.

My body was made just for me.

Food is not the enemy.

My body is a temple.

I accept my body as is.

I am just enough as I am.

What do you love about your body?

When you feel insignificant:

I am worthy of love.

I am enough.

If people criticize me, I can survive that. Nothing says that I have to be perfect.

Hey, you're awesome! Keep it up!

I am surrounded by peaceful people.

People treat me with kindness and respect.

All of my relationships are positive and filled with love and compassion.

You are beautiful.

I am open and willing to attract all that I desire, beginning here and now.

If you're not receiving the same energy you put into a friendship or relationship, leave. You are not a doormat.

Add affirmations that make you feel significant:

When you are conflicted about a decision:

I know my inner self will guide me in the right direction.

When you focus on what you want, everything else will fall in place. Stay focused.

All good things are coming to me.

I release all things that no longer benefit me: objects, ideas, habits, or relationships.

I find opportunities to be kind and caring everywhere I look.

I think only about what I can do right now. By thinking small, I accomplish great things.

Add affirmations for when you are confused:

When you can't sleep:

I release all emotional negativity.

I am free to be in the present moment.

As I inhale peace, I exhale to release.

I have done my best today, and I am willing to forget the rest.

Nighttime is my time to heal.

I have done my best today, and I am willing to forgive the rest.

I am thankful for the chance to close my eyes.

Add affirmations to help you go to sleep:

When you worry about your future:

The future is good. I look towards it with hope and happiness.

I am worthy of my very best life.

I have so much potential.

I am attracting good things in my life.

I will accept and embrace everything that happens.

I will face any obstacle with courage and wisdom.

I have infinite patience when it comes to fulfilling my own destiny.

I believe in what's possible.

I am a divine creation, a piece of God. How can I be undeserving?

Add affirmations about your future:

When you come face to face with a problem:

It's ok to not be ok.

I can talk to someone to help me out without being judged.

I have the wisdom to know what to change.

I release what no longer serves me.

This too shall pass.

I only desire things that are healthy for me.

You are not alone.

Add affirmations for when you feel troubled:

When you feel you are not good enough:

I fully approve of who I am, even as I get better.

I am more than good enough, and I get better every day.

I am the best me there is.

I choose my own path and worth.

I am a purposeful daughter.

I need you to survive.

My thoughts and feelings are nourishing.

So many people love you. Don't focus on the people who don't.

You are the Goddess of your own life, the creator of your own dreams. You're more than enough!

Add affirmations for when you feel alone:

When you feel that you have failed:

I have good ideas.

My biggest dreams can come true.

I will overcome my mistakes.

I believe in my dreams.

I have a great imagination.

Anything I dream of is possible.

I am creative.

I can reach my dreams.

I am in charge of my future.

Every problem has a solution.

Add affirmations to encourage yourself:

Add all the pictures you want

Crisis Hotlines

EMERGENCY - 911

Rape Crisis Center - 702-385-2153

Depression Hotline - 1-800-273-8255

Drug Abuse Hotline - 1-855-516-1669

Suicide Prevention Hotline
1-800-273-8255
Or Text: ANSWER to 839863

Homeless Hotline - 1-866-827-3723

www.PurposefulDaughter.org

Copyright © 2020

All rights reserved. No part of this publication may be reproduced, distributed, or transmitted in any form or by any means, including photocopying, recording, or other electronic or mechanical methods, without the prior written permission of the publisher except in the case of brief quotations embodied in critical reviews and certain other noncommercial uses permitted by copyright law.

For permission, requests, and speaking engagements:

Contact: www.purposefuldaughter.org
Facebook: Facebook.com/groups/PurposefulDaughter
Instagram: @PurposefulDaughter
ISBN: 978-0-578-68755-1

www.ingramcontent.com/pod-product-compliance
Lightning Source LLC
Chambersburg PA
CBHW062021290426
44108CB00024B/2738